BEI GRIN MACHT SICH IHR WISSEN BEZAHLT

AF131221

- Wir veröffentlichen Ihre Hausarbeit,
  Bachelor- und Masterarbeit

- Ihr eigenes eBook und Buch -
  weltweit in allen wichtigen Shops

- Verdienen Sie an jedem Verkauf

Jetzt bei www.GRIN.com hochladen und kostenlos publizieren

Bibliografische Information der Deutschen Nationalbibliothek:

Die Deutsche Bibliothek verzeichnet diese Publikation in der Deutschen National-bibliografie; detaillierte bibliografische Daten sind im Internet über http://dnb.d-nb.de/ abrufbar.

Dieses Werk sowie alle darin enthaltenen einzelnen Beiträge und Abbildungen sind urheberrechtlich geschützt. Jede Verwertung, die nicht ausdrücklich vom Urheberrechtsschutz zugelassen ist, bedarf der vorherigen Zustimmung des Verlages. Das gilt insbesondere für Vervielfältigungen, Bearbeitungen, Übersetzungen, Mikroverfilmungen, Auswertungen durch Datenbanken und für die Einspeicherung und Verarbeitung in elektronische Systeme. Alle Rechte, auch die des auszugsweisen Nachdrucks, der fotomechanischen Wiedergabe (einschließlich Mikrokopie) sowie der Auswertung durch Datenbanken oder ähnliche Einrichtungen, vorbehalten.

Impressum:

Copyright © 2016 GRIN Verlag, Open Publishing GmbH
Druck und Bindung: Books on Demand GmbH, Norderstedt Germany
ISBN: 9783668338920

Dieses Buch bei GRIN:

http://www.grin.com/de/e-book/338742/computer-use-in-teaching-and-learning-in-kenya-physical-infrastructure

Beatrice Ngeno

Computer use in teaching and learning in Kenya. Physical infrastructure and resource availability

GRIN Verlag

GRIN - Your knowledge has value

Der GRIN Verlag publiziert seit 1998 wissenschaftliche Arbeiten von Studenten, Hochschullehrern und anderen Akademikern als eBook und gedrucktes Buch. Die Verlagswebsite www.grin.com ist die ideale Plattform zur Veröffentlichung von Hausarbeiten, Abschlussarbeiten, wissenschaftlichen Aufsätzen, Dissertationen und Fachbüchern.

Besuchen Sie uns im Internet:

http://www.grin.com/

http://www.facebook.com/grincom

http://www.twitter.com/grin_com

ASSEMENT OF PHYSICAL INFRASTUCTURE AND RESOURCE AVAILABILTY THAT SUPPORTS COMPUTER USE IN TEACHING AND LEARNING IN AINAMOI SUB-COUNTY,KERICHO COUNTY, KENYA

(Beatrice Chebet Ngeno)

University of Kabianga

Abstract

Education which is integrated with technology is very vital and globally networks the education globally. Physical infrastructure and availability of resources that supports computers use in teaching and learning public primary schools is issue that should be address to in Kenyan educational and dynamic world trends. The study set out to access the physical infrastructure that supported computer use in the public primary school in Ainamoi sub county Kericho county. The Research design used for this study was descriptive survey design. A total of 42 teachers and 21 head teachers participated in the study. 2 ICT Experts and Dquaso officer participated in the study. Information was collected using questionnaires, structured interviews, observations and checklist. Data analysis was presented in tables and percentages. Findings reveal that the electricity, ICT designed classrooms and computer labs were that were available physical infrastructures that supports computer use. Based on the findings, the suggestions were that the government to increase FPE allocation to allow schools to purchase sufficient computers.

Table of Contents

List of abbreviations & acronyms

CEO	County of Education Office
DQUASO	District Quality Assurance and Standards Officer.
D'v S	Digital Versatile Disks
E.C.D.E	Early child hood and education.
F.P.E	Free primary education.
ICT	Information Communication Technology
ICTI	Information Communication Technology Integration
IWB	Interactive White Board
KEMI	Kenya Management Institution
KIE	Kenya Institute of Education
MOE	Ministry of Education
MOEST	Ministry of Education and Technology.
P.T.E	Primary Teachers' Examination.
TPACK	Technological Pedagogical and Content of Knowledge
TSC	Teacher Service Commission
UNESCO	United Nation Education Science Cultural Organization

Definition of terms

E-learning - Refers to teaching and learning that is facilitated under computer mediated environment.

Information communication Technology - (ICT) refers to equipment such as computers, televisions and digital cameras that are used to support head teachers work.

Information Technology (IT) - refers to the art of managing and processing information using computer technology, computer hardware, software and accessories that are used to accomplish a task

Instructional Media - It's an approach or a technique which I used in teaching and learning.

Integration - To combine two or more things so that they may work together. Computer to be combined with teaching and learning so that it may work better.

Preparedness - Refers to how conversant or readiness to use the skills, knowledge and attitude one has acquired during training or studies and is competent to use computers.

Introduction

The emergence of knowledge based society, pupils and adults learning in cyber cafes are becoming emerging issues in the education sector. Global competition is faced by world people seeking education which is computer integrated based. According to according to Kamal (2009) noted that with the advent of computers and technological advances like the internet, the face of education World over has changed, be it at school education, higher education, teachers training or distant education, the use of technology in some form.

Globally, there is a higher competition based on knowledge acquisition. World Bank (1995), states that the emergence of a global knowledge based on economy being accompanied by increasing willingness by governments to invest in education. This indicates that the World Bank assists countries to get into Information and Communication Technologies (ICT's) so as to contribute to education goals, achievements and improve standards of living. World Bank (1995), states that the emergence of a global knowledge based on economy being accompanied by increasing willingness by governments to invest in education. In this case the World Bank is helping countries to get into Information and Communication

The Indian government made significant progress in achieving the goals of using computers in public schools and came up with a policy framework based on the use of computers and focused initiatives. These include the Computer each schools Scheme geared towards making opportunities available to students and school administrators for developing their Computer skills at the school level. Hawlerdge (1990) stated that, almost all teachers and head teachers use computers in public schools in the developed countries.

According to MINECOFIN (2001), the government of Rwanda is striving to achieve this through the in-service of teachers through the institutional programmes such as Kigali Institute of Education that had launched computer programmes to upgrade the skills on computer use of the under-qualified teachers.

In Kenya, National Council for Science and Technology (2010) stated that, providing teachers and other educational professionals with access to and use of Computers is one key component to developing the necessary human capital which the education sector requires for the wide adoption of technology. This will improve the effectiveness in teaching and learning because school dropouts and absenteeism will be minimized. This will motivate the learners and encourage participation. According to Nepad – E –(2005 to 2006) Schools demonstration project, attempts to set computers basic infrastructures in public primary school in Kenya but was negligible. This is so due to lack of computers, low computer literacy level among teachers, fear by the school administrators that computers require high level personnel to operate and lack of electricity in schools and high cost of computers. The community does not give computer purchase and installation in schools as a priority. Therefore, it is important for the Kenya Government to allocate enough and improve the physical infrastructure to embrace the technology. Nyambane at el (2014) found that there are numerous factors that influence teachers' use of computers.

Records at Kericho District Education Office indicated that there were 131public primary schools. There were no clear records showing physical infrastructure and resource availability that supports computor use in Ainamoi sub-county given that computer usage in public primary schools is a matter of serious concern. In the view of the importance of education, to the community and the nation at large.

Statement of the Problem

There was need to improve the quality of school teaching and learning in public primary schools. Computer is perceived as a necessary tool for this purpose. ICT policy of 2006, the government has made effort to integrate ICT in education. To achieve this objective, the Ministry should employ strategies and ways such as; improving ICT physical infrastructure that supports computer use in public primary schools, equipping education institutions with ICT equipment and to train or develop the capacities of education teachers in the use of computers in teaching and learning. Since quality education is a right to every Kenyan child the Kenyan Government requires that all children get the relevant and reliable education recognized globally. The use of computers had proofed to be effective in daily work. (World Bank 2002).Computer software gives public primary teachers a wide range of options on helping them to perform differently in teaching and learning. Little has been done on the role of computer technology on teacher's preparedness and resources availability in computer use in teaching and learning in public primary schools; particularly in areas Such as Ainamoi Sub County, Hence this study, intended to find out the physical infrastructure and resource availabity that supports use of Computers in teaching and learning processes in public primary schools in Ainamoi Sub County, Kericho County.

The research questions was that which physical infrastructures available, that support computer use in the public primary schools in Ainamoi Sub- County?

Significance of the Study was that the findings and recommendations will be beneficial to the Ministry of Education, Science and Technology (MOEST), School Administrators, teachers and learners to employ effective integration of computers in teaching and learning process and thus meet the academic current global trends. Also findings will be beneficial to curriculum developers in digital curriculum content to integrate successful primary education.

Scope of the Study was responses sought to obtain through two ICT experts draw from Kericho teachers college in form of interviews and observations. The DQUASO officer was interviewed to formulate recommendations.

Theoretical framework

In this study The Technology Acceptance theory is applied. Its proponent was Davis in 1989. This is an information systems theory that models how users come to accept and use technology. The model suggests that when users are presented with a new technology, a number of factors influence their decision about how and when they will use it (preparedness), notably: Perceived usefulness (PU) defined by Fred Davis (1989) as the degree to which a person believes that using a particular system would enhance his or her job performance. Perceived ease of use defined by Davis (1989) as the degree to which a person believes that using a particular system would be free from effort. For our study the Teachers preparedness in the use of Computers in public primary schools will be enhanced by improved teaching and learning and would use little effort when using IT in their teaching/learning and administrative tasks. Criticisms of Technology Acceptance.

Model as a theory include its questionable heuristic values, limited explanatory and

Predictive power, triviality, and lack of any practical value (Chuttur, 2009).

Literature review

According to a study done by Tubin and Chen, (2002) in Israel, found that an essential aspect of a new model for computer integration in primary school teaching was to establish a broad computer infrastructure and provide every teacher a laptop computer .

A study done in Rivers State of Nigeria by Achuonye (2012) on Comparative Study of Computer Literacy in Urban and Rural Primary Schools found that learning environment on every Computer Science class in rural schools, takes place in the classroom 240(100%) and never in any designated equipped room called Computer Lab. He added that this case is only slightly different in urban areas because 32(13%) use computer lab while the majority, 208(87%), do not.

A study carried out by Farrell (2007), pointed out that transportation of imported equipments, tariffs charged for electricity added to the cost thus making ICT unaffordable to many schools. Access to internet services for more utilization of computers in the learning process was particularly expensive for many schools.

A study carried out in Bondo County in Kenya by O. Isaiah (2013) on the head teacher preparedness in use of ICT found that all the head teachers and teachers found that Out of 240 respondents from rural and urban areas respectively, only 80(33%) rural respondents indicated that there are computers in their schools while 160(67%) were on the contrary, but all the 240(100%) urban respondents admitted that there are computers in the urban schools. The 80(33%) rural respondents that have computers in their schools responded to issues on teachers' accessibility to computers as never (0(0%) rarely (16(20%), seldom (40(50%) and often (24(30%), always (0). Similarly, their urban colleagues responded: never (16(7%), rarely (63(26%), seldom (96(40%), often (65(27%), and always (0(0%).

A study done by Muigai (2011) found that there are dozens of challenges facing implementation in Kenya such as lack of qualified teachers to ICT in schools, lack of computers, lack of electricity, the cost of computers burglary and the fear of teachers being rendered irrelevant. .

A study carried out by- Laaria Mingaine – 2013 in Challenges in the Implementation of ICT in Public Secondary Schools found that, it was evident that generally, electricity supply was not a barrier to ICT implementation in schools. However, there were instances where respondents felt that limited supply of power was an impediment to ICT implementation. In such situations there was a likelihood of limited rural electrification or frequent power disruptions and this could slow down the pace of ICT implementation in schools. He further added that, alternative sources of power such as generators, solar technology and batteries should be explored in the absence of the electric power.

A study done by Zakawa. P. (2013) in Jimeta on evaluation of computer studies discovered that most of the schools have not yet introduced the teaching and learning of computer education as a subject .The schools where computer education is being taught, there are no enough computers for students' practical, no qualified computing personnel, and sometimes these schools are faced with the problem of erratic electricity supply.

A study done by Nchunge, Sakwa, & Mwangi, (2013) in Kiambu County on Assessment of ICT Infrastructure on ICT Adoption in Educational Institutions: pointed out that connectivity and network infrastructure as hindered full access to internet resources, e-mail use and re-source sharing in schools in Kenya. The above were done in different countries and those studies done in Kenya was done in different subjects the current study differed from the current study because the study was carried out in Ainamoi sub county in public primary schools in use of computers. The physical infrastructure found to be supporting the use of computers in teaching and learning was relevant to the current study hence shown the appropriate physical infrastructure necessary to be used to supported computer use.

Descriptive research was used in the study. (Kothari 2004) noted that Descriptive research includes descriptive surveys and facts findings and inquiries of different kinds.

The study was done in Ainamoi Sub-county, Kericho County. This Sub County was made up of both rural and urban public primary schools hence Kericho town central business location was found there. Schools were located in four administrative sub-locations namely; Municipality zone covering both urban and rural regions, and the purely rural areas of Ainamoi zone, Kapsaos zone and Kapsoit zone with each being administered by a Zonal Quality Assurance and Standards Officer (ZQASO). The researcher chose the area because variety of teachers works there. The researcher choice the study area since Kericho teachers training college was located in Ainamoi Sub County where the ICT experts were drawn from.

Ainamoi Sub-County Division had 68 public schools and 31 private schools that have presented candidates for KCPE (Kericho Sub County Education Office Report, 2014). It was centrally positioned among the eleven divisions that form Kericho County.

The study population was drawn all the public primary schools in the Ainamoi Sub -County that were registered and are enrolled up to class 8 The DQASO officer and 2 ICT experts from Ainamoi Sub County education and Teachers Training College respectively was interviewed.

The study population was 68 public primary schools in Ainamoi Sub- County. A representation in form of a percentage was then used to sample each zone. Orodho and Kombo (2002) argue that at least 30% of the target population is considered ideal as this facilitated generalization of the finding.

Ainamoi Sub -County. Sample Size

Zone	Public Schools	Sampled Schools (30%)
Municipality	12	4
Ainamoi	18	5
Kapsaos	16	5
Kapsoit	22	7
Total	68	21

Source: Author (2014)

Mugenda and Mugenda (2003) noted that the goal of stratified sampling is to achieve desired representation from various sub-groups in the population. Random sampling also was appropriate for the study since teachers in schools was picked randomly from the stratified sampling. Using purposive sampling, the researcher selected 4 schools from Municipality zone, 5 schools from Ainamoi zone, 5 schools from Kapsaos zone, and 7 schools from Kapsoit zone. Therefore the research involved 21 out of 68 public primary schools, thus represented 30% of the study population. From each of the 21 schools, purposive sampling was used in selecting lower primary teachers. Simple random sampling was used to select 2 lower primary teachers as participants in the study, making a total of 42 teachers hence it included one head teachers per school in every zone.

Secondly, from the 21 schools, the researcher employed stratified sampling to select 1 school from Municipality zone, and 2 schools each from Ainamoi zone, Kapsaos zone, and Kapsoit zones, making a total of 7 schools to be used conducting. Mugenda and Mugenda (2003) 10% - 30% is a good representation of the target population. Data Collection Instruments was Questionnaire. Questionnaire is widely used frequently in the descriptive research because they obtained facts about current conditions and are useful in making inquiries concerning their views and opinions (Mugenda & Mugenda, 2003). The instrument was selected because it gave the respondent adequate time to give the relevant information required and made it possible for anonymity. The Head teacher and the lower primary public school teachers were administered with the questionnaires. The questionnaires were both open ended and close

10

ended so that each question gathered all information. The Interview schedule was used to gather information from the DQASO and 2 ICT experts. The entire ICT expert was drawn from Kericho teachers Training College. The Interview was where the respondent was asked a series of questions depending on the information required (MC Burney & White, 2010). Observation schedule was also used to confirm the teacher's information. According to Mc Burney and White (2010) observation involves recording ongoing behavior without attempting to influence it. This also implies to collection of information by way of own investigation without interviewing the respondent (Orodho, 2004). This was important in the study because the researcher observed what was happening without manipulating the outcome.

According to Reliability and validity are measures of relevance, stability and consistency of data collection procedures. (Simiyu & Opiyo, 2011), Validity of a measurement instrument was the extent to which the instrument measured what was supposed to measure. Validity takes different forms, each of which is important in different situations (Mugenda & Mugenda, 2003 and Orodho, 2004).

Reliability of instrument

Reliability of a measurement instrument is the extent to which it yields consistent results when the characteristic being measured has not changed (Mugenda & Mugenda, 2005). Test – retest reliability will be adopted in this study because the instrument will be administered on different occasions in period of two week. The instrument will be administered to the same respondent twice at an interval of two weeks. Two weeks will be found to be standard for these instruments to pilot (Mugenda & Mugenda, 2003

Data analysis involved editing, organizing and summarizing the information obtained through questionnaires and interview schedules. The data collected was analyzed using calculate percentages, and frequencies of respondents and tables

Results and Presentation on physical infrastructure on resource availability that supports computer use

This part reports on findings from all the three instruments of the study which are; the questionnaire, interview schedules and observation and the observation checklist. The head teachers and teachers' questionnaire was the primary instrument.

Head Teacher and Teacher response on physical infrastructure that supports computer use

List of physical infrastructure.	Available and adequate	Available and not adequate	Not Available and not adequate	Remarks
1.Computer laboratories	6(14.28%)	36(85.72%)		Not available
2.Designed ICT classrooms	24(57%)	14(33.34%)	4(9.52%)	Available and not adequate
3.Elecctricity	38(90.47%)		4 (9.52%)	Available
4.Generators		2(4.76%)	40(95.24%)	Not available
5.Solar	4(9.52%)	16(38.10%)	22 (52.38%)	Not available
6.Computers	4(9.52%)	6(14.28%)	32(76.19%)	Not available
7.Electricity cables	34(80.95%)	8(19.04%)		Available
8.Printer	8(19.04%)	12(28.57%)	11(52.38%)	Not available
9.Power point machine		2(19.04%)	34(80.95%)	Not available
10.Photocophy machine	8(19.04%)		34(80.95%)	Not available
11.Well secured classroom	20(47.61%)	18(42.85%)	4(9.52%)	Available and not adequate
12.Slides	-	2(2.38%)	40(97.62%)	Not available
13. Internate	-	-	42(100%)	Not available
14.Others	-	-	42(100%)	Not available

The physical infrastructure that was reported to be available and adequate was Electricity which were indicated by 38 respondents were 90.47%, Electricity cables were indicated by 34 respondents which represented by 80.95%. Designed ICT classrooms were indicated by 24 respondents which represented 57.00%.Secured classroom were 20 respondents which represented 47.61%. Physical infrastructures that were indicated to be available and not adequate were found to be; Computers labs were indicated by 36 respondents which represented 85.72%. well secured classrooms were indicated by 18 respondents which were 42.85%. The ones who had solar were 16 respondents represented 38.10% .Designed ICT classrooms were indicated by 4 respondents which were 33.34%.

The ICT2 Expert also gave the similar physical infrastructure that supports computer use in teaching and learning in that:

Computer laboratories or ICT Designed classrooms should be well constructed, ventilated and connected with extension cables. Provide world class ICT facilities that include but not limited to: smart and high speed laptops, internet connectivity and infrastructure. Provide special education software's that include: e-softwares, digital/virtual libraries, e-encyclopedia, wiki conferences, movies/videos, YouTube etc to facilitate sharing of content.

Physical infrastructures that were indicated to be not available and not adequate were found to be: internet connection indicated by 42 respondents which were 100%. Slides which were indicated by 40 respondents representing 97.62%.The schools which had no generators were 40 respondents representing 95.24%. Photocopy machine, were indicated by 34 respondents which were represented by 80.95%. Power point machine were indicated by 34 respondents which were represented by 80.95%. Those schools with computers were indicated by was indicated by 32 respondents represented 76.19%. Solar had 22 respondents representing 52.38%.

From the teachers training college the researcher observed that they had a well facilitated ICT room. The room had 52 computers which were on use, well connected with extension cables and reliable internet. They had printers, photocopier machines, power point machines and projectors which were well maintained. During the observation period, the researcher observed that first year class which was FH was in session and the computer basic skills were being taught.

From the sampled public primary schools the researcher found that more than 80% public primary schools were well connected with power which was functioning. The schools that had no power were in the programme by the government that by the end of this year, those schools without power will be connected. The ICT designed classroom and computer rooms were also there in some of the schools. They were not adequate due to the large numbers of enrollment in public primary schools.

To determine the level of infrastructure that is available and that can support the teaching and learning process of public primary school in Ainamoi Sub-County the research focused on Computers Laboratories, Designed ICT Classrooms, Electricity (main power), Generators, Solar, Computers, Electricity cables, Printer, Power point Machine, photocopy machine well secured classroom, Internet connection, Slides and others. Of this physical infrastructure electricity, designed ICT classrooms and well secured are the most available physical infrastructure that support computer use in most of the public primary school. Electricity connections in

13

most of the schools were well connected Computer laboratories or ICT Designed classrooms should be well constructed, ventilated and connected with extension cables.

The ICT .1. expert noted that: Provide world class ICT facilities that include but not limited to: smart and high speed laptops, internet connectivity and infrastructure .provide special education software's that include: e-softwares, digital/virtual libraries, e-encyclopedia, wiki conferences, movies/videos, YouTube etc to facilitate sharing of content. The infrastructure as shown is still limited to fully use computers in the public primary school in Ainamoi Sub-County. The lack of computers, internet access and other essential cause a hindrance to these schools from using computers in teaching and learning.

DQUASO officer added that: Basically electricity connections have been done in most of the public primary schools which was funded by the government. ICT designed classrooms are already constructed in some of the schools. Computers have not been purchased by the government but some schools have bought theirs privately or supported by donors and sponsors.

The above study is in agreement with the studies carried out by Mingaine (2013) who noted that electricity supply was not a major barrier to ICT implementation in schools just as it is presented in the findings which shown that of the entire infrastructure, electricity was the most available and accessible. Nchunge, Sakwa, & Mwangi, (2013) pointed out that connectivity and network infrastructure as hindered full access to internet resources, e-mail use and resource sharing in schools in Kenya. Baylor and Ritchie (2002) found that teachers valued the use of instructional technologies in the classroom and that it had positive impact on students' content acquisition and class performance.

The physical infrastructure that was reported to be available and adequate was Electricity connection and Designed ICT classrooms. Physical infrastructures that were indicated to be available and not adequate were found to be; Computers labs and well secured classrooms. From the ICT Expert also gave the similar physical infrastructure that supports computer use in teaching and learning in that: Computer laboratories or ICT Designed classrooms should be well constructed, ventilated and connected with extension cables

Provision of world class ICT facilities that include but not limited to: smart and high speed laptops, internet connectivity and infrastructure. Provision of special education software's that include: e-softwares, digital/virtual libraries, e-encyclopedia, wiki conferences, movies/videos, YouTube etc to facilitate sharing of content should be also be provided.

Physical infrastructures that were indicated to be not available and not adequate were found to be: internet connection, Slides, generators, Photocopy machine, Power point machine, Solar From the teachers training college the researcher observed that they had a well facilitated ICT room. They had printers, photocopier machines, power point machines and projectors which were well maintained.

Summary

The ICT designed classroom and computer rooms were also there in some of the schools. They were not adequate due to the large numbers of enrollment in public primary schools. The ICT Expert also indicated that, to determine the level of physical infrastructure that is available and that can support the teaching and learning process of public primary school in Ainamoi Sub-County the research focused on Computers Laboratories, Designed ICT Classrooms, Electricity (main power), Generators, Solar, Computers, Electricity cables, Printer, Power point Machine, photocopy machine well secured classroom, Internet connection, Slides and others. Of this physical infrastructure electricity, designed ICT classrooms and well secured are the most available physical infrastructure that support computer use in most of the public primary school. Electricity connections in most of the schools were well connected Computer laboratories or ICT Designed classrooms should be well constructed, ventilated and connected with extension cables.

The ICT expert noted that: Provide world class ICT facilities that include but not limited to: smart and high speed laptops, internet connectivity and infrastructure .provide special education software's that include: e-softwares, digital/virtual libraries, e-encyclopedia, wiki conferences, movies/videos, YouTube etc to facilitate sharing of content.

The infrastructure as shown is still limited to fully use computers in the public primary school in Ainamoi Sub-County. The lack computers, internet access and other essential cause a hindrance to these schools from using computers in teaching and learning.

Conclusions

It was clear that the physical infrastructure that supports computer use in teaching and learning in public primary schools are wanting given that computers labs or ICT designed classrooms should be expanded due to the high enrolment of pupils. Computers should be purchased which should be sufficient in appropriately integration in teaching and learning.

Recommendations

In light of the research findings, the researcher wishes to make the following

1. The ministry of education should put in place the ICT maintenance schedule upon introduction of computer integration. Since no school had incorporated computer technology in their current Teaching and learning programs, it was recommended that computer labs be constructed so that it will gather for the entire class one through class eight pupils. This will be important to have to engage consistence computer integration in teaching and learning in public primary schools.

2. The Ministry of Education should develop a policy of curriculum digital content guide which will enable the teacher to integrate computers successful in teaching and learning. Teachers to be provided with professional opportunities in areas of computer technology through regular capacity building courses, workshops and seminars. Teacher training institutions (universities and other Teacher Training Colleges) should evaluate how teacher trainees who are future teachers could be prepared to be computer literate and make computer course to be KNEC examinable.

Suggestions for Further Research

Further research could be done on:

1. Similar research could be carried out in other Sub- County to compare notes.

2. A study on the role of computer technology on general teaching and learning process.

3. The extent of which schools management and administration supports computer integration in education in the County.

References

Farrell, G & Isaacs, S (2007). *Survey of ICT and Education in Africa: A Summary Report, Based on 53 Country Survey.* Washington, DC: infoDev/ World Bank. Retrieved from http://www.infodwev.org/en/Publication.353.html

G.O.K. (2006). *The National information and communication technology policy.*

Haddad, W.D. and Draxler, A. (2005). *The dynamics of technologies for Education.*

Howridge, K. (1990). *Creating a technology rich constructivist environment in a class Information Technology.*

Komal, K. L. (2009). *Understanding teachers and administrators perceptions and compute integration in education.*

Kothari, C.R. (2004). *Research methodology.* Methods and techniques (2nd revised

Laaria Mingaine (2013) *School of management Research journal of social science and management learning*, 12(4), 199-204.

MC Burney, D.H & White, T.L (2010). *Research methods.* Wardsworth Cengage Learning United States of America.

MINECOFIN (2007c) *National Guide for Planning, Budgeting and Policy Review*, Republic of Rwanda, Kigali.

Ministry of Education, Kenya (2012). *ICT integration in education,* Ministry of Education. Nairobi. Government Printers.

MOE (2013). *Kericho District Educational Day.* Prepared by DEO's Office Kericho.

Mugenda, O.M & Mugenda, A.G (2003) *Research Methods: Quantitative and Qualitative Approaches Nairobi:* ACTS Press.

Mwalongo, A. (2011). *Teachers' perception about ICT, professional development, administration and personal use.* Dar el Salam University College, Tanzania

Nchunge,M. D., Sakwa, M. & Mwangi, W. (2013). Assessment of ICT Infrastructure on ICT Adoption in Educational Institutions: A Descriptive Survey of Secondary Schools in Kiambu County Kenya. *Journal of Computer Science & Information Technology 1*(1). pp. 32-45

Nkpa, M. (1997). Educational Research for Modern Schools; fourth edition: No.5 *International Online Journal of Educational Sciences, 2009, 2*(1), 81-97 - Investigation of Teachers' Computer Usage Profiles and Attitudes toward Computers - Tamer KUTLUCA (2009)

Nyambane C.O and Nzuki,D.(2014). *Factors Influencing ICT Integration in Teaching.*

Orodho, J.Aand kombo (2002). *Techniques of Writing Research Proposal and Reports in Education and Social Sciences.* 5th edn. Mosola Publishers, Nairobi. (2008 edition). Techniques of Writing Research Proposal and Reports in Education and social sciences. 5th edn. Mosola publishers, Nairobi

Oulo I. O. (2013). *Preparedness of The Head teachers In The Use Of Information Communication Technology In Public Primary Schools In Bondo District, Kenya.* Unpublished Research Report of the University of Nairobi.

Tubin, D., & Chen, D. (2002). School-based staff development for teaching within computerized learning environments. *Journal of Research on Technology in Education, 34* (4), 517–528.

Weng, C.H. & Yang, Y.T.C. (2009). *A Successful Technology Integration in Schools to Improve the Effectiveness of Elementary School Administration.* Chinese Government Printers.

World Bank, (1995). *Applying New Technologies and Cost-Effective Delivery Systems in Basic Education.* World Economic Forum, Dakar.

World Bank. 2002. *Globalization, growth, and poverty: building an inclusive world economy.* A World Bank policy research report. Washington, D.C.: The World Bank. http://documents.worldbank.org/curated/en/2002/01/1683370/globalization-growth-poverty-building-inclusive-world-economy